Finished Already?

Constructive Activities for Students Who Finish Early

Grades 5-6

by
Linda De Geronimo
and
Anne Diehl

Carson-Dellosa Publishing Company, Inc.
Greensboro, North Carolina

Credits

Editor

Amy Gamble

Layout Design

Amy Gamble

Inside Illustrations

Mike Duggins

Cover Design

Peggy Jackson

Cover Artist

Dan Sharp

ISBN 0-88724-973-6

Table of Contents

Theme Three: The World Around Us

Theme Four: Brainteasers and Puzzles

Introduction

You have completed the instruction portion of your lesson, and your students are doing independent practice. You see a few hands start waving in the air and hear the echo of voices repeating, "I'm done. What do I do now?" The time you had allotted for the activity is not up yet and you're wondering, "How can they be finished already?" Sound familiar?

Most students finish their work at about the same time, but there are always a few who can whiz through their work in an exceptionally short period of time. Busy work is not productive, so it is certainly not the answer. *Finished Already?* provides students with a variety of standards-based activities to complete during any downtime in their days. As students complete these creative and meaningful activities, they will be challenged to use higher level thinking skills and to draw on prior knowledge and experiences.

Most of the activity pages are written so that you will need to provide few extra materials and little or no instruction. For those activities that do require materials or instruction, simply use a few minutes prior to your lesson to demonstrate the procedure for completing the activity. For your convenience, any material setup that may be required is mentioned in a *Teacher Note* at the bottom of the page. To avoid confusing the students, that portion of the page may be cut off. Ideas for use and organization of the activities are outlined on the following pages.

Your students will enjoy the fun activities in *Finished Already?,* and you will enjoy the tremendous progress your students make throughout the year as they use their free time productively.

Organization Tips

Depending on your learning climate and classroom-management style, you may choose to present individual pages as needed or you may want to have a variety of pages available daily. Either way, setup and preparation will be the same. Set aside a corner of your room where all types of manipulatives and art supplies (cubes, discs, buttons, straws, glue, paper, etc.) can be stored in labeled bins. Reproduce the activity pages and make them available in baskets or envelopes in this same area. Include a list of materials for each activity on the front of the envelope or basket. This will enable students to gather supplies before returning to their work areas. It's also a good idea to have empty baskets available for students to transport the supplies they will need. Once finished with an activity, students should be responsible for returning the supplies used to the appropriate supply bins. Students' completed work can be collected in another bin or envelope in this same area.

To avoid having to make numerous copies, activity pages with no need for written responses can be made into pocket folder activities. Simply staple or glue one copy of the activity to the inside of a pocket folder. Then, gather the materials needed for the activity and place them inside a resealable plastic bag. Tuck the bag inside the folder's pocket. You may want to create a set of three to five folders for each activity so that more than one student can work on a given activity at one time.

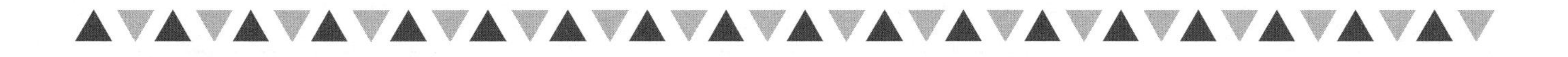

You may, instead, elect to create centers around your room. Most activities can be used in a writing, math, or free center. The materials required to complete the activities should be at the center so that once students visit the center, they will not need to move around the room to gather supplies.

A writing center should contain writing paper, construction paper, pencils, markers, etc., set up in bins, baskets, cans, or on shelves. A dictionary should also be handy. The math center should be set up in a similar manner and should contain a variety of manipulatives, including buttons, cubes, number and operation tiles, a balance scale, plastic coins, dice, paper, etc. The free center could include magazines, an almanac and other reference books, and any other special materials needed for the activities.

It is important for students to understand that the activities, although entertaining and fun, are academic in nature and that you expect them to take their work seriously. This can be accomplished by setting the stage for learning as you present the activities and then by maintaining records to identify students who frequently use the activities. An easy way to keep track of this is to post a chart, like the one included on page 62, identifying the activities and names of students so that they can check off and date when they finish an activity. This will give you a running record of which students in your class are using their time wisely.

Name ______________________________ Date ____________________

A Story Web

Directions Select the most recent fiction book you have read and create a story web by filling in the diagram below with details about the character(s), setting(s), problem(s), and solution(s).

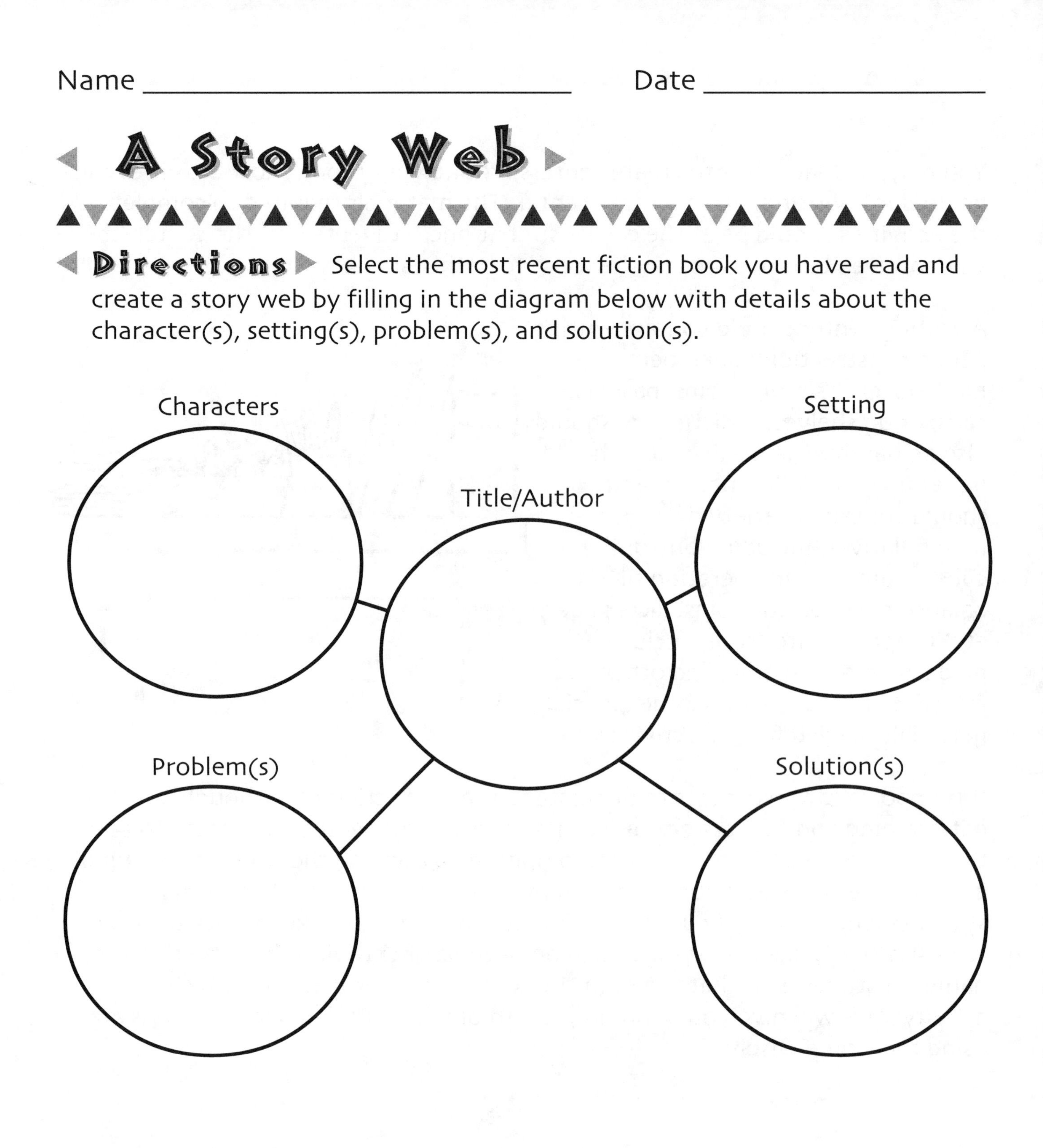

Bonus Use the information that you listed above to create an interesting book jacket. Design an attractive cover that includes the title of the book and the author's name. On the back, add a brief summary without revealing the ending. Also, tell about the author.

Name ______________________________ Date ____________________

A Picture Book

Directions Create a picture book to share with a younger student. Select a novel that you think would interest a younger student if it was rewritten with easier words. Consider the illustrations that could help tell the story.

Draw pictures on separate sheets of paper that match the sequence of events in the story and help the reader understand the plot. Add a simple sentence or two to describe the action. Make sure you present the characters, setting, problem(s), and the solution(s) within your pictures and text.

Bonus Share your simple version of a favorite novel with a young reader.

Name ______________________________ Date ____________________

Bumper Stickers

Directions People often put bumper stickers on their vehicles to promote something they believe in or enjoy. Create your own bumper stickers to promote one of the following: your school, your country, conservation, equal rights, democracy, free choice, or a topic of your choice.

Bumper stickers catch a person's eye if they are colorful, attractive, and make a point with few words. Some phrases even rhyme. Check out the examples below to get you started. Write and decorate your bumper stickers on the strips provided.

Bonus Develop a plan to sell your bumper stickers. Who would want to buy them? Where would you sell them? For how much?

Teacher Note: Provide sentence strips or strips of plain paper.

Name ______________________________ Date ____________________

Time in a Bottle

Directions Pretend that you have been asked to gather items to bury in a bottle as a time capsule on school grounds. You are to select ten items that best represent your school population and significant occurrences during the last five years. Think about the last five years and important school, local, and national events that occurred during this time period. You may need to complete research to collect this data. Now, make a list of items you would like to bury in a time capsule or bottle. From your list, select the top ten choices. Remember: They must fit in a bottle no bigger than a gallon milk jug. Draw the ten items you have selected in the bottle below.

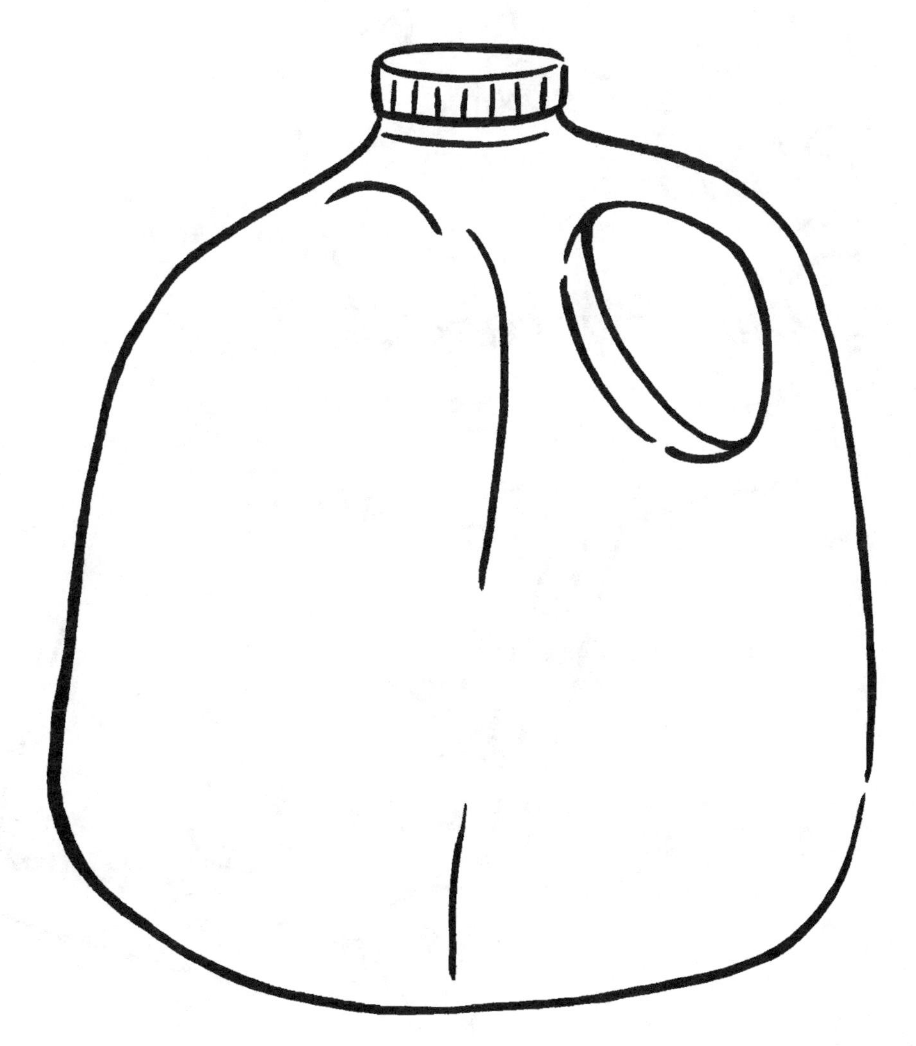

Bonus Explain why you selected each item.

Name ______________________________ Date ____________________

What's in a Name?

Directions Write your name vertically down the left side of a large sheet of paper. Think of things that are special to you. Also think of things that you do well or that you like. Use each letter in your name to write a word or phrase that best describes you as a special, unique person. Decorate your poster with things that you like. Make it bright and cheerful.

Bonus Make a name poster for a friend or family member.

Name ______________________________ Date ____________________

A Story Pyramid

Directions Create a story pyramid by using the prompts below to share information about a favorite book.

1. Name of the book
2. Two words describing the setting
3. Names of three main characters
4. Four words describing the main characters
5. Five words stating the problem
6. Six words describing the rising action
7. Seven words describing the climax
8. Eight words describing the descending action
9. Nine words describing the ending
10. Ten words describing your opinion of the book

1. ______________________________

2. ______________ ______________

3. ____________ ____________ ____________

4. __________ __________ __________ __________

5. ________ ________ ________ ________ ________

6. _______ _______ _______ _______ _______ _______

7. ______ ______ ______ ______ ______ ______ ______

8. ______ ______ ______ ______ ______ ______ ______ ______

9. _____ _____ _____ _____ _____ _____ _____ _____ _____

10. _____ _____ _____ _____ _____ _____ _____ _____ _____ _____

Name ______________________________ Date ____________________

Personification Personified

Directions Personification is a writing technique that authors use when they give inanimate objects the ability to talk. What if the objects that you use in school had the ability to talk for one day? What would they say about you, your school, your classmates, and their own responsibilities and circumstances? First, describe each object's character traits. Then, give each a voice. For example, your pencil might be a little grumpy because of all the writing it must accomplish in English class. It might not appreciate the pencil sharpener and complain bitterly. It might have opinions about what you are making it write. Give it a try. Personify the following items and see what they have to say: a pen, your left shoe, your wristwatch, your writing journal, your binder, your locker, your desk.

____

____

____

____

____

____

____

____

____

____

____

____

____

____

____

____

____

Name ______________________________ Date ____________________

Become a Playwright

Directions Try your hand at writing a play. A play is really just a story that is acted out in front of an audience. First, think of something you would like to write about. Your story could be about a real event or something fictional. Think of familiar stories. This will help you decide on a topic.

Topic/Main Idea: ______________________

____

____

Now, follow the steps below to get started.

1. Create a story action list or a sequence of events.
2. Set the scenes by dividing your story into sections according to each new action.
3. Create the settings to show where and when things occur.
4. Give your characters dialogue, or something to say to each other, to tell the story.
5. Determine what stage directions are needed to move your characters around.
6. Read your play and revise as needed. (When you read and revise, make sure your play is simple to follow and the settings, scenes, and character dialogues all match and make sense.)

Bonus Draw a storyboard (a series of pictures) to show several different scenes or the main events in your play.

Name ______________________________ Date ____________________

Write a Myth

Directions The people of ancient Greece made up stories to explain the unknown, such as why the sun rises and why the weather changes. These stories are called myths. These myths told of gods and goddesses who ruled the earth with extraordinary powers. Read the example of a myth below, then write your own. Think of the forces of nature (hurricanes, tidal waves, lightning, tornadoes, rainstorms, sunrise, sunset, etc.). Choose a force of nature to explain with a myth and follow the graphic organizer below to help write your myth.

Example: Persephone, the daughter of Demeter, the goddess of agriculture, is kidnapped by Pluto, the god of the underworld. Persephone is allowed to return to her family for half of every year. For the half of the year that she is in the underworld, Demeter is very sad and therefore will not allow anything to grow on the earth until her daughter is returned to her. This explains fall and winter. When Persephone returns to her family during spring and summer, Demeter is happy and allows plants to bloom and grow again.

What force of nature will you explain?	
Who are your characters?	
What is the plot?	
What are the problems in your story?	
How does your story end?	
How is the force of nature explained?	

Name ______________________________ Date ____________________

Write a Limerick

Directions A limerick is a form of poetry that is usually funny. Limericks have five lines. Lines one, two, and five of the poem rhyme. Lines three and four also rhyme. Limericks are fun to read aloud because they have a rhythm—lines one, two, and five have three stressed syllables, and lines three and four have two. Read the limerick below and stress each syllable that has an accent.

There ónce was a mán named Jóe

Who wánted to áct in a shów.

He tríed for a párt,

He lóved with his héart,

But he fróze when they tóld him to gó.

Now, try to write a limerick of your own.

____

____

____

____

____

Bonus Draw a picture to go with your limerick.

Name ______________________________ Date ____________________

Say It Again

Directions Synonyms are words that have the same meaning as another word. Some synonyms for the word *house* are *abode, domicile, dwelling, home,* and *residence.* Knowing synonyms for a word can improve your writing by making it more interesting (so that you don't use the same words over and over again). Learning synonyms will also expand your vocabulary, which is always a good thing.

Find the correct synonym for each word below. All words have more than one right answer. Try to do as many as you can without any help. If you get stuck, use a dictionary or a thesaurus to help. Draw lines from each word on the left to its synonyms on the right.

car	educate
	beginning
book	tome
	intelligent
birth	putrid
	depiction
trip	journey
	portrayal
smart	irate
	congenial
teach	sharp
	reply
nice	start
	pleasant
bad	automobile
	decayed
answer	instruct
	respond
mad	volume
	angry
picture	expedition
	buggy

Bonus Write ten sentences using synonyms that you just learned.

Name ______________________________ Date ____________________

Comic Strip Fun

Directions Comics are fun to read. They can also be fun to create. Invent your own cartoon character, then write your own comic strip.

Use the space below to draw your main characters. You may use people, animals, or a combination of both. Try to give your characters personality by using facial expressions and clothing. You don't have to be an artist to be successful; many comic strip characters are drawn very simply.

Hi!

Now that you have created your characters, use speech bubbles to give them words and try putting them in the comic strip frames below.

Name ______________________________ Date ____________________

Fun with Idioms

Directions An idiom is a phrase or saying that has a different meaning (figurative) than what the actual words mean (literal). For example: *"He's in the doghouse"* literally means that someone or something is actually in a real house made for a dog. But, what we really mean, or the figurative meaning, is that someone's in trouble for doing something wrong.

Choose an idiom from the list below and draw and color a picture of its literal meaning and figurative meaning.

1. He was shaking in his boots.
2. He lost his marbles.
3. He has a splitting headache.
4. He almost jumped out of his skin.
5. You're driving me up the wall.
6. Don't cry over spilled milk.
7. It's raining cats and dogs.
8. She's a pain in the neck.
9. There is a fork in the road.
10. We see eye to eye.
11. She was walking on air.
12. Hold your horses!
13. She blew the test.
14. He is full of beans.
15. Lend me a hand.
16. Cat's got your tongue.
17. It's on the tip of my tongue.
18. Straight from the horse's mouth.
19. Two heads are better than one.
20. She has a green thumb.

Bonus Can you think of any other idioms? Draw and label another picture. Try one more!

Name ______________________________ Date ____________________

Talk to the Author

Directions Wouldn't it be great to tell your favorite author what you think of his or her last book? Write a letter to that author. Address each prompt below to create the body of your letter. Go on-line or visit the library to get the author's mailing address and send him or her your letter. Who knows? You might just get a response!

1. I like/dislike your story because …
2. I like/dislike the main character because …
3. I like/dislike the sequence of events because …
4. The setting is important because …
5. The character I like the most is … because …
6. The character most like myself is … because …
7. I wish you had …
8. I don't understand why …
9. I find the book too easy/hard to read because …
10. The story reminds me of …
11. The story is interesting/boring because …
12. The strongest part of the story is …
13. The weakest part of the story is …
14. I think the purpose of this book was …
15. The most amazing thing I learned was …
16. I found the vocabulary in the book to be …
17. If I could write a different ending, I would …
18. A good sequel for this book would be …
19. If I were you, the next book I would write would be about …
20. The final question I have is …

Bonus Pretend you are the author and received the letter you just wrote. How would you respond? Write a letter responding to your original letter.

Name ______________________________ Date ____________________

All about Me

Directions An autobiography is a story that a person writes about his or her own life. You will create your own time-line autobiography.

- Think about the major events in your life (birth, first words, first day of school, etc.).
- Fill in the time line below with these events and corresponding dates.
- Use a piece of large white construction paper to create your final time line.
- Select small coins (if available) with dates that match the major events marked on your time line. You do not need one for each event.
- Glue the coins where they belong on the time line.
- Write a sentence or two describing each event.
- Draw or bring in pictures for each event to display on the time line.
- Decorate your time line with things you love.
- You may add more lines as you need them.

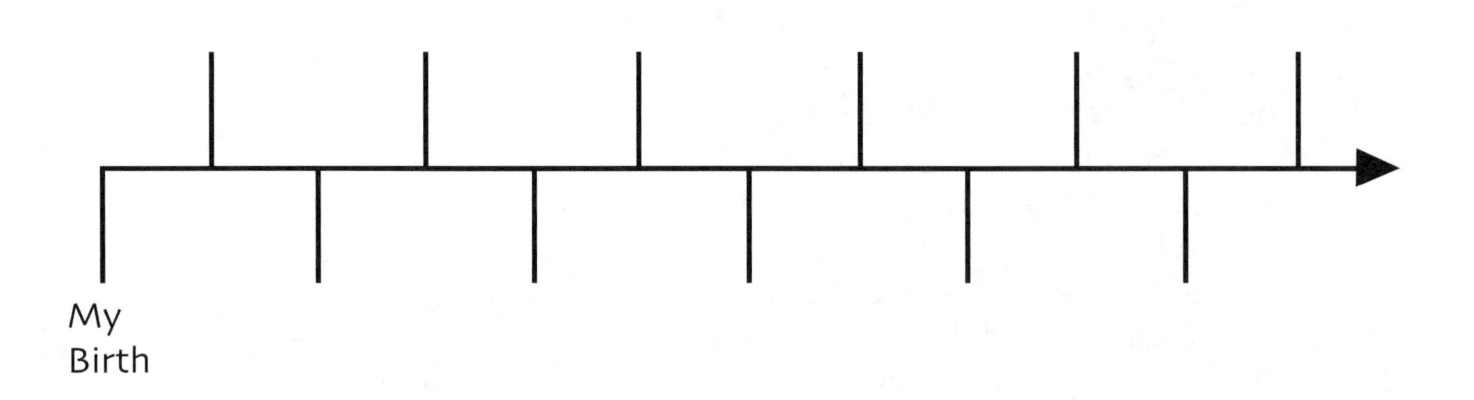

My
Birth

You can make extra lines on your time line and add more paper to it as each new major event happens to you. You can hang your time-line autobiography in your room until high school graduation!

Teacher Note: Provide large white construction paper and, if possible, small coins.

Name ______________________ Date ______________

Division Riddles

Directions Solve the division problems below. Then, find each answer at the bottom of the page and write the corresponding letter on the line above the number. If your problems are all correct, you should be able to answer the riddles at the bottom of this page.

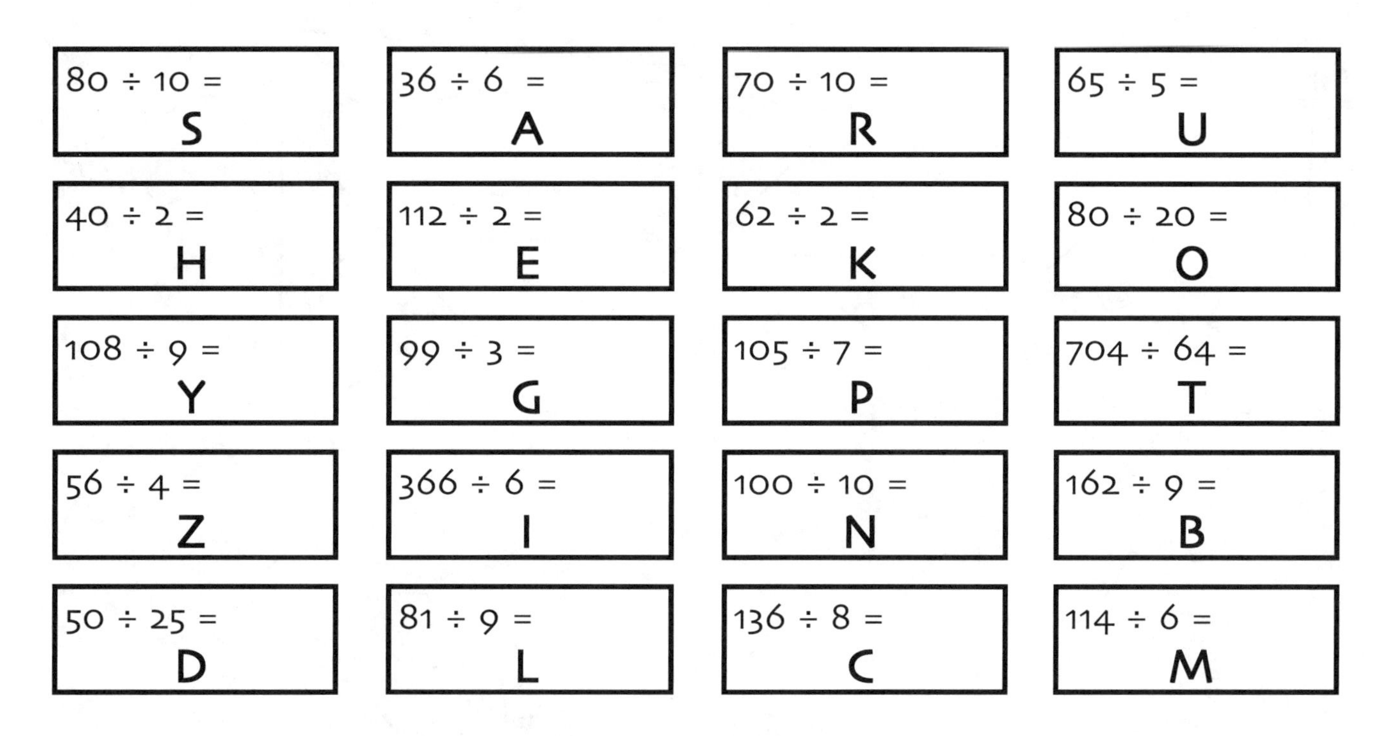

80 ÷ 10 = S	36 ÷ 6 = A	70 ÷ 10 = R	65 ÷ 5 = U
40 ÷ 2 = H	112 ÷ 2 = E	62 ÷ 2 = K	80 ÷ 20 = O
108 ÷ 9 = Y	99 ÷ 3 = G	105 ÷ 7 = P	704 ÷ 64 = T
56 ÷ 4 = Z	366 ÷ 6 = I	100 ÷ 10 = N	162 ÷ 9 = B
50 ÷ 25 = D	81 ÷ 9 = L	136 ÷ 8 = C	114 ÷ 6 = M

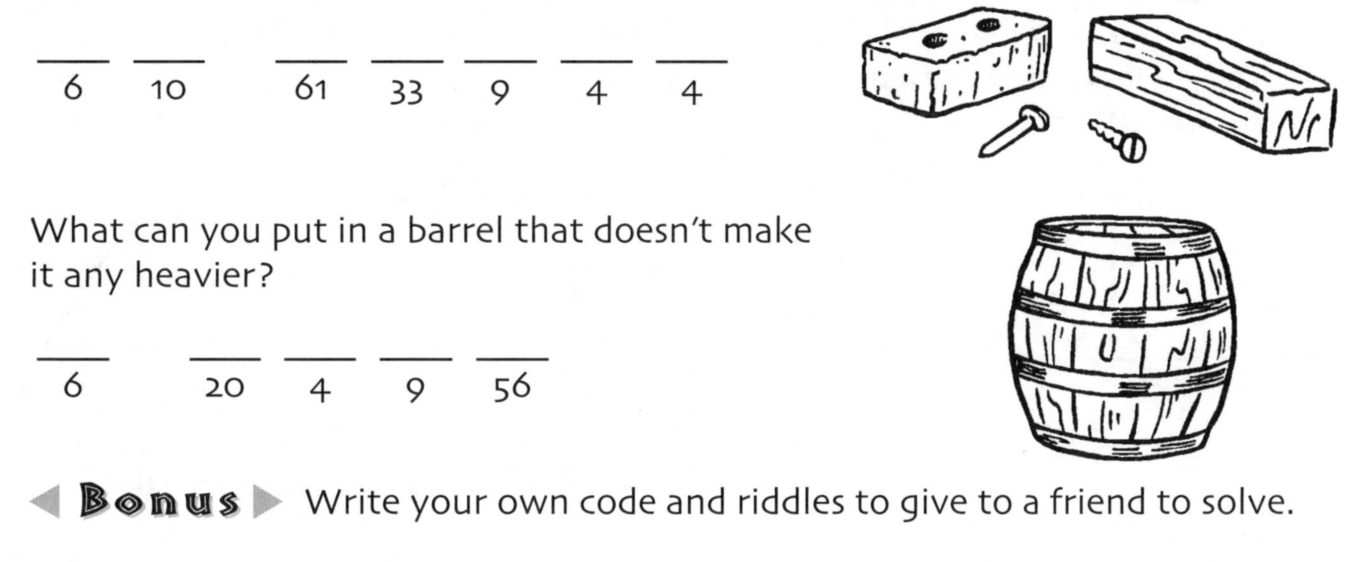

What kind of house has no bricks, wood, nails, or screws?

___ ___   ___ ___ ___ ___ ___
6 10   61 33 9 4 4

What can you put in a barrel that doesn't make it any heavier?

___   ___ ___ ___ ___
6   20 4 9 56

Bonus Write your own code and riddles to give to a friend to solve.

Name ______________________________ Date ____________________

Piece It Together

Directions All triangles have three inside angles. The sum of all three angles always equals 180°. Match up the triangle pieces below to form complete triangles with three angles that add up to 180°. Color all the pieces that go together with one color. Use another color for the next set and so on.

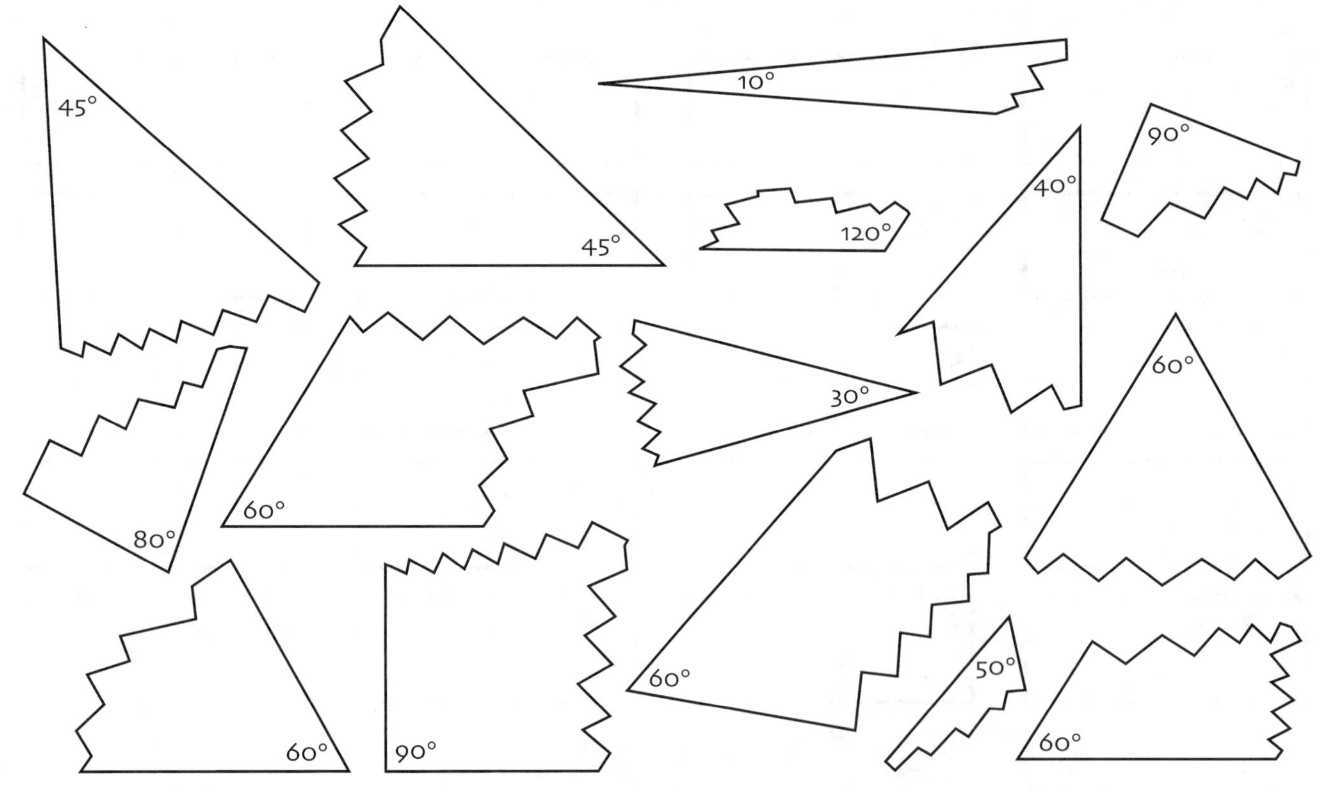

Bonus Angles or sides can classify triangles. Below are three triangles that are named for the characteristics of their sides and one triangle named for its angle. Hint: The first letter of each name (from left to right) will spell the word RISE.

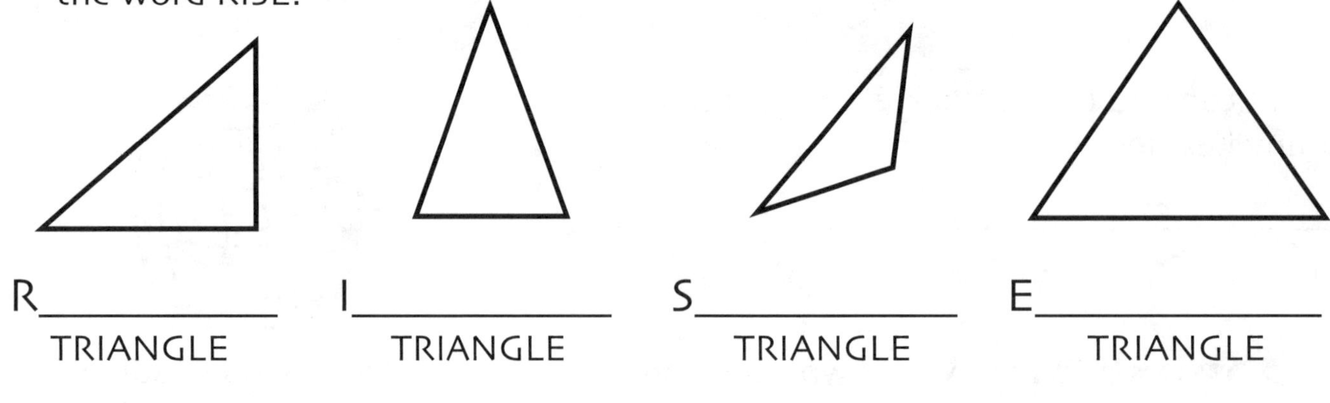

R____________ I____________ S____________ E____________

TRIANGLE TRIANGLE TRIANGLE TRIANGLE

Name ______________________ Date ______________

Division Made Easy

Directions Become a division whiz by using the chart below to help you divide large numbers.

A number is divisible by 2 if ...	the number in the ones column is an even number.	45,852 yes 45,851 no
A number is divisible by 3 if ...	the sum of the numbers is divisible by 3.	456: 4+5+6=15 15 is divisible by 3
A number is divisible by 4 if ...	the last two numbers form a number that can be divided evenly by 4.	616 yes 622 no 16 ÷ 4 = 4 22 ÷ 4 = 5 R2
A number is divisible by 5 if ...	the number in the ones column is a 5 or a 0.	550 yes 3,415 yes 481 no
A number is divisible by 6 if ...	the number is also divisible by both 2 and 3.	534 yes 252 yes 391 no
A number is divisible by 9 if ...	the sum of the numbers is divisible by 9.	4,896 yes 308 no 4+8+9+6=27 3+8=11
A number is divisible by 10 if ...	the number in the ones column is 0.	480 yes 631 no

Circle every number in each row that can be divided by the first number.

2	24	153	802	4,003	6,008	10,231	_____
3	21	31	108	4,188	8,008	11,322	_____
4	21	36	124	438	1,816	40,850	_____
5	15	105	244	651	1,003	10,485	_____
6	31	64	132	4,221	6,060	16,002	_____
9	28	63	108	2,484	9,000	18,468	_____
10	101	435	680	4,430	10,820	122,661	_____

Add the numbers that you circled in each row and write your answer on the line. Next, add those sums to find one big sum. My answer is ________________.

The answer you find should be a palindrome (a word or number that reads the same backwards and forward, like Anna and 61,216).

Bonus Write other math problems that have palindrome answers.

Name ______________________________ Date ____________________

Find the Perimeter

Directions The distance around an object is the perimeter. Find the perimeter around the outside of the figure below. Use your knowledge of geometry to help you.

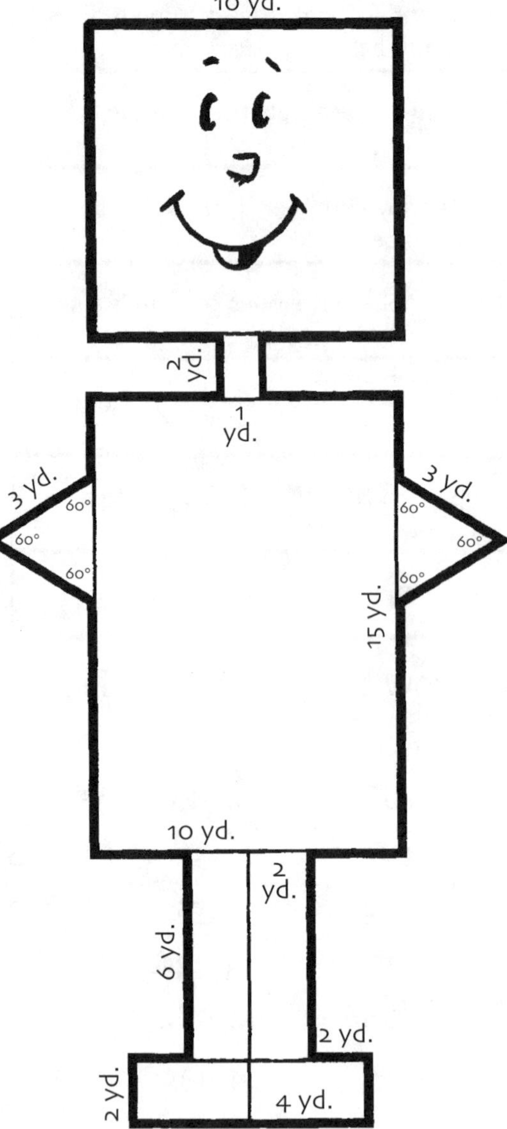

Bonus Check your answer. Change the perimeter from yards to feet and then change your answer from feet to inches.

If your answer is 4,392 inches, your calculations were correct. Congratulations! If not, try again.

Name ______________________ Date ________________

Flying High

Directions Arrange the numbers from the list below with a combination of operation signs (+, -, x, ÷) so that your final answer is 100. Starting at the bottom, write a number or operation sign on each line in the rocket. You must use each sign at least once and each number only once. The first one has been done for you.

1	10	35
2	11	50
~~5~~	15	50

Don't give up. Keep trying—this can be tricky!

Bonus How many ways can you find for these same numbers to work?

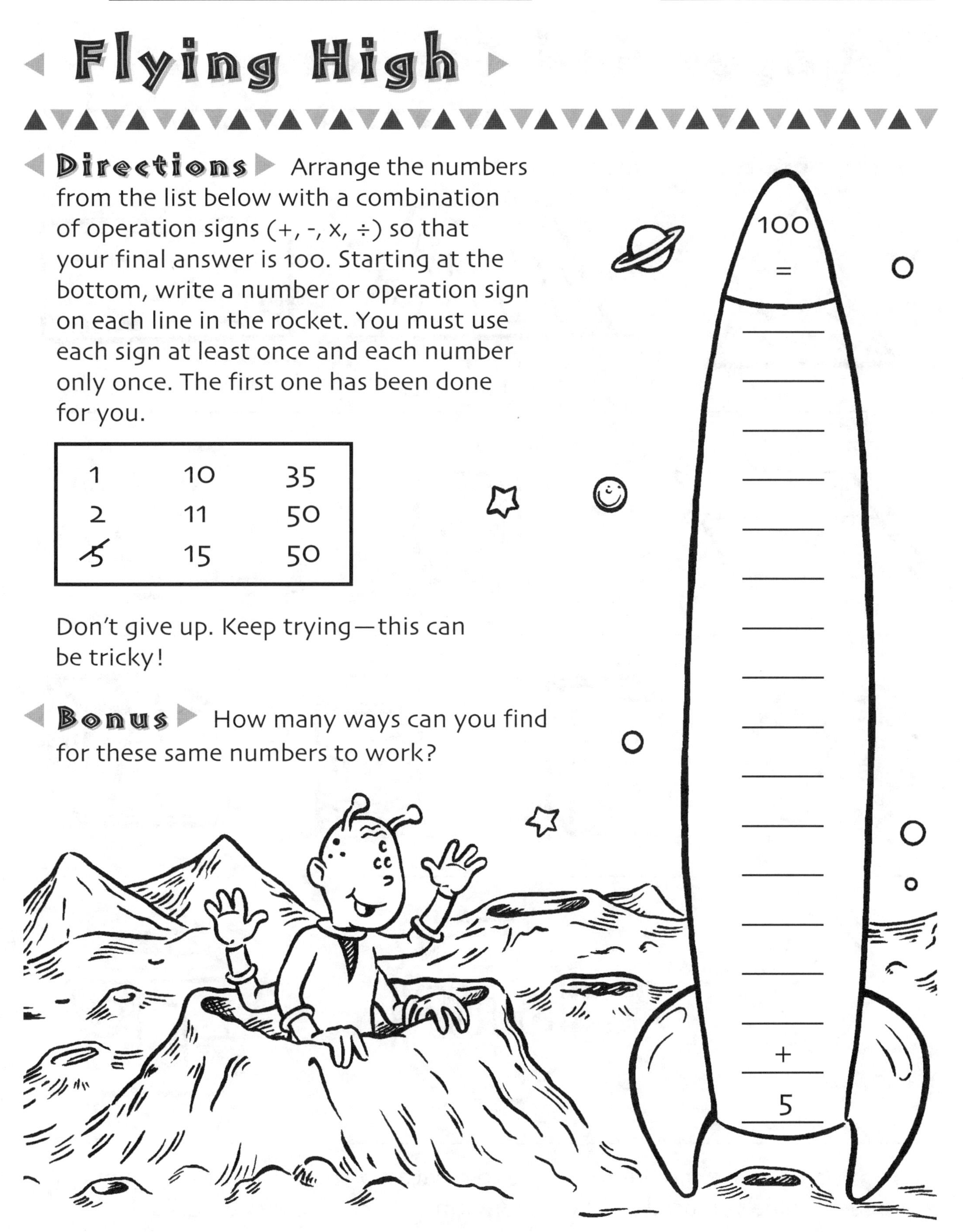

Name ______________________ Date ______________________

Shapes and Scenes

Directions Name the shape of each bold figure below.

Bonus Use the figures above to create a picture. Identify the number of each shape you used and how many times each one was used.

Name ______________________________ Date ____________________

Hidden Math

Directions Can you find all the math terms from the Word Bank hidden in the picture below? Circle and label them in the picture.

Word Bank

square	addend	median	sphere	congruent	percent
triangle	diameter	equal sign	mean	octagon	parallel
product	rectangle	subtrahend	symbol	acute angle	sum

The Princess and the Pea

STOP

Before you leave.... Remember your homework!

1. 4826 + 3972 = 8798

2. 3829 × 7 = 26803

3. 6789 − 482 = 6307

10"

C x D = π

Grades

70

98

65

76

85

83

94

81.57%

A B C 1 2

Kyle

Name ______________________________ Date ____________________

It's My Flag

Directions Design a new flag for your family. Be sure to follow the directions below. Be creative and try to design a pattern that would make your flag interesting.

- Select at least three colors that represent your family.
- Select one design that best describes your family (hearts, basketballs, music, etc.).
- Color $\frac{1}{2}$ of your flag the first color you chose.
- Color $\frac{1}{9}$ of your flag the second color you chose.
- Color $\frac{1}{4}$ of your flag the third color you chose.
- Draw the design you chose in $\frac{5}{36}$ of your flag.

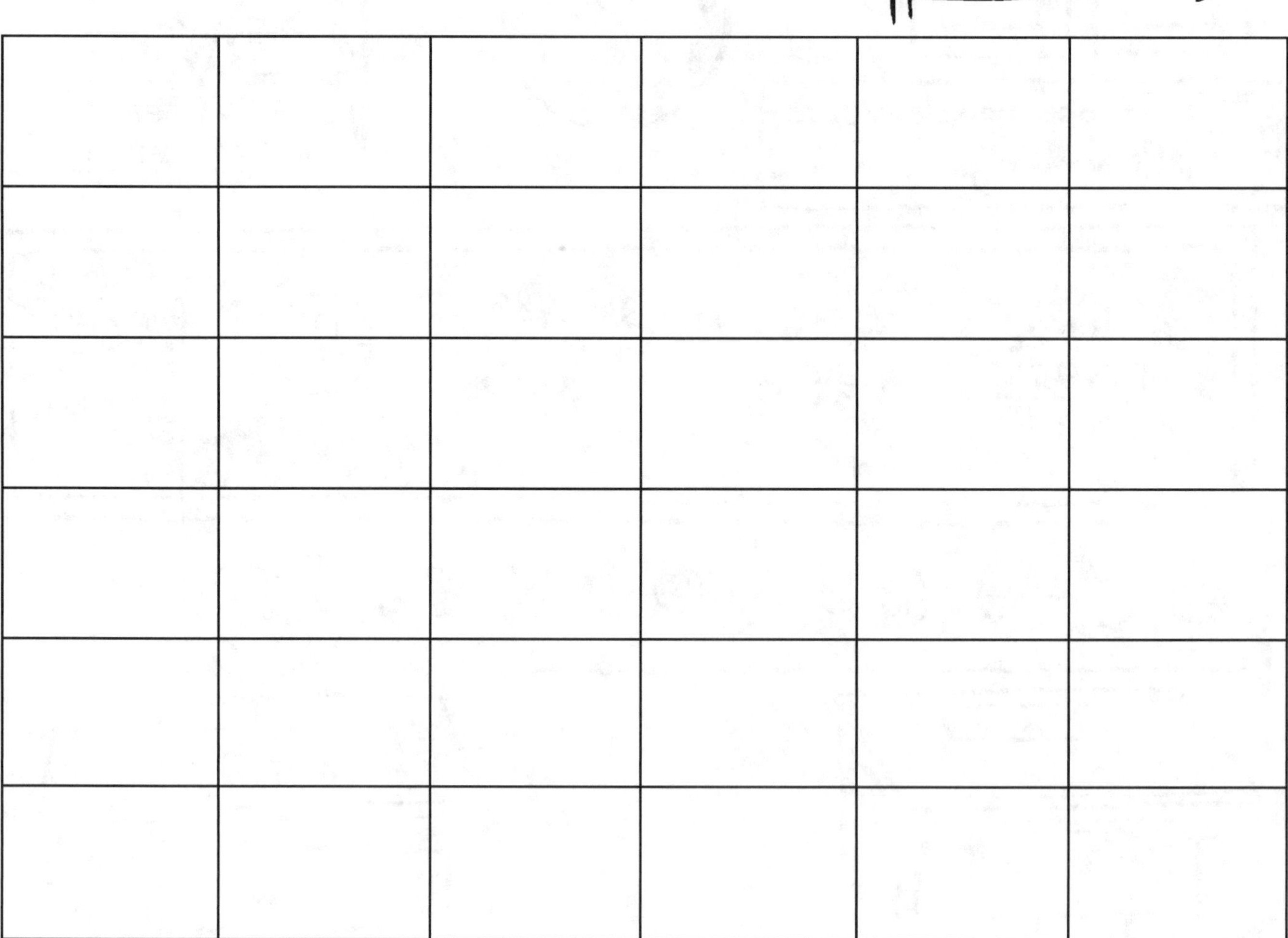

Name ______________________ Date ______________

Think Math!

Directions Below you will find a list of incomplete words that relate to math. Try to fill in the blanks to complete each math word. The list starts with an *a* word and continues to *z*.

a __ d __ __ d
b __ r r __ __
c __ __ g r __ __ __ __
__ a __ a
e __ __ __ t __ __ n
f __ c __ __ __
__ r __ __ h
h __ x __ __ __ __
i __ f __ __ __ t __
j __ __ n
k i __ __ g r __ __
__ e __ g __ h
__ e __ n

n __ m __ __ __
__ __ d
__ __ __ __ __ l l __ l
q __ __ t i __ __ t
r __ __ __ u s
s __ l __ t __ __ n
__ __ s s __ l l __ t __ __ n
u n __ __
v __ __ t __ x
w __ __ g h __
x – a __ __ s
__ a r __
z __ r __

Choose ten words from above and show examples of each term in picture form. The first one has been done for you.

1. *odd:* ______________________
2. ______________________
3. ______________________
4. ______________________
5. ______________________
6. ______________________
7. ______________________
8. ______________________
9. ______________________
10. ______________________

Name ______________________________ Date ____________________

Delicious Fractions

Directions On the lines below, write the approximate fraction shown in each picture of the recipe.

______ of a head of lettuce

______ cup of black olives

______ of an apple

______ of a carrot

______ of a green pepper

______ tomatoes

______ of a cup of croutons

______ of a cucumber

Bonus Take this recipe home and, with the help of an adult, make a Fabulous Fraction Salad by combining the ingredients above. Serve the salad with your favorite salad dressing.

Name ______________________ Date ______________

Find the Order

Directions Pretend that your friend Jill must visit town and has several errands to do. Jill has a long shopping list and she needs to save time.

Read Jill's shopping list below and study the location map on page 34. Help Jill plan the quickest way to complete her shopping trip by listing the stores she needs to visit in the most efficient order.

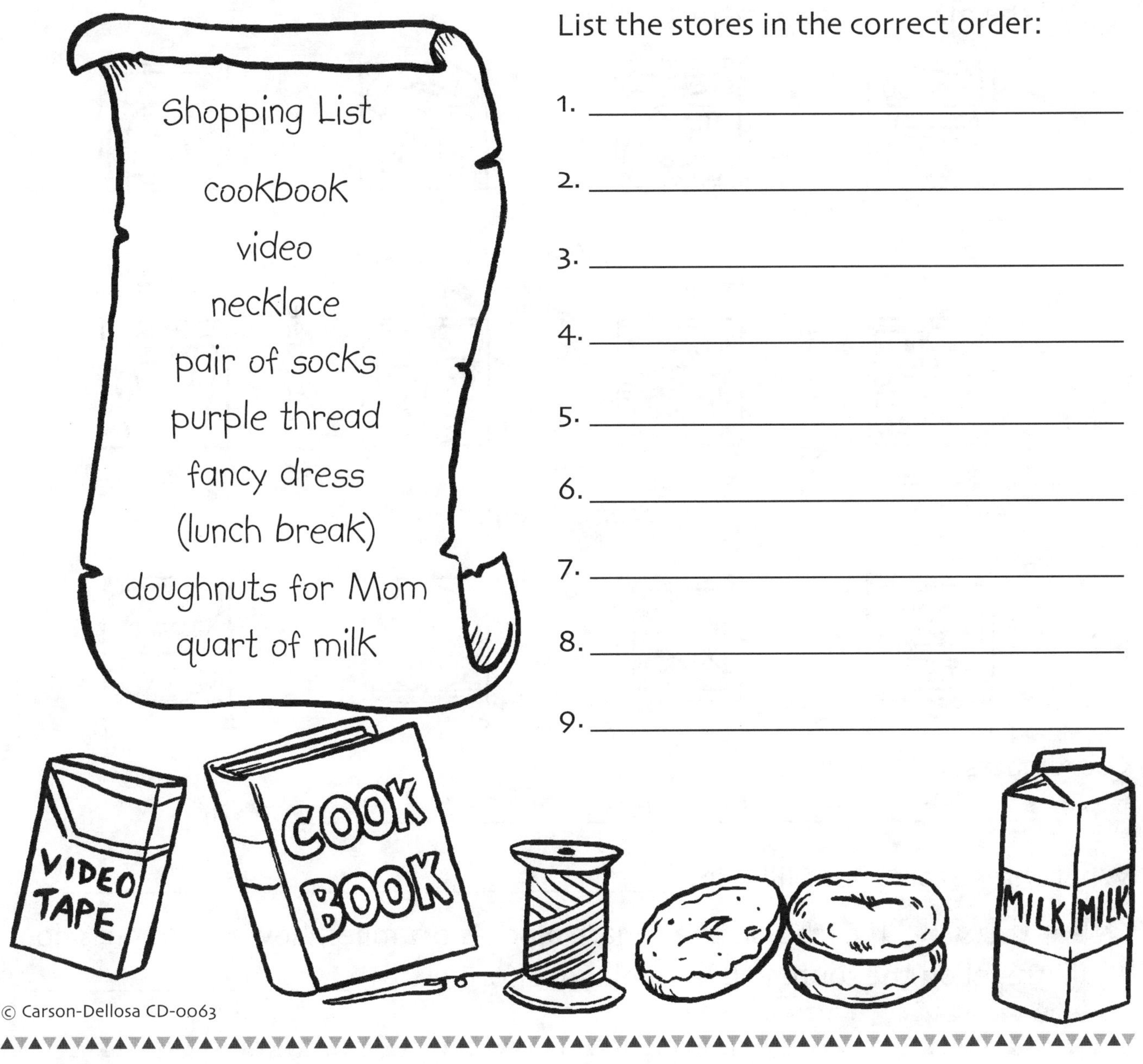

List the stores in the correct order:

1. ______________________
2. ______________________
3. ______________________
4. ______________________
5. ______________________
6. ______________________
7. ______________________
8. ______________________
9. ______________________

Teacher Note: Provide copies of page 34.

Name ______________________________ Date ____________________

Give the Coordinates

Directions Jill is using this location map to find the stores for her shopping trip. Review the items on Jill's shopping list (page 33), then name the coordinates for each store in the most efficient order. Jill starts on Main Street at coordinate 4A, visits eight more coordinates, then returns to 4A. She must remain on the sidewalks and crosswalks (no cutting across diagonally), she may enter a store from any corner (but must exit from the same corner), and she may have to backtrack.

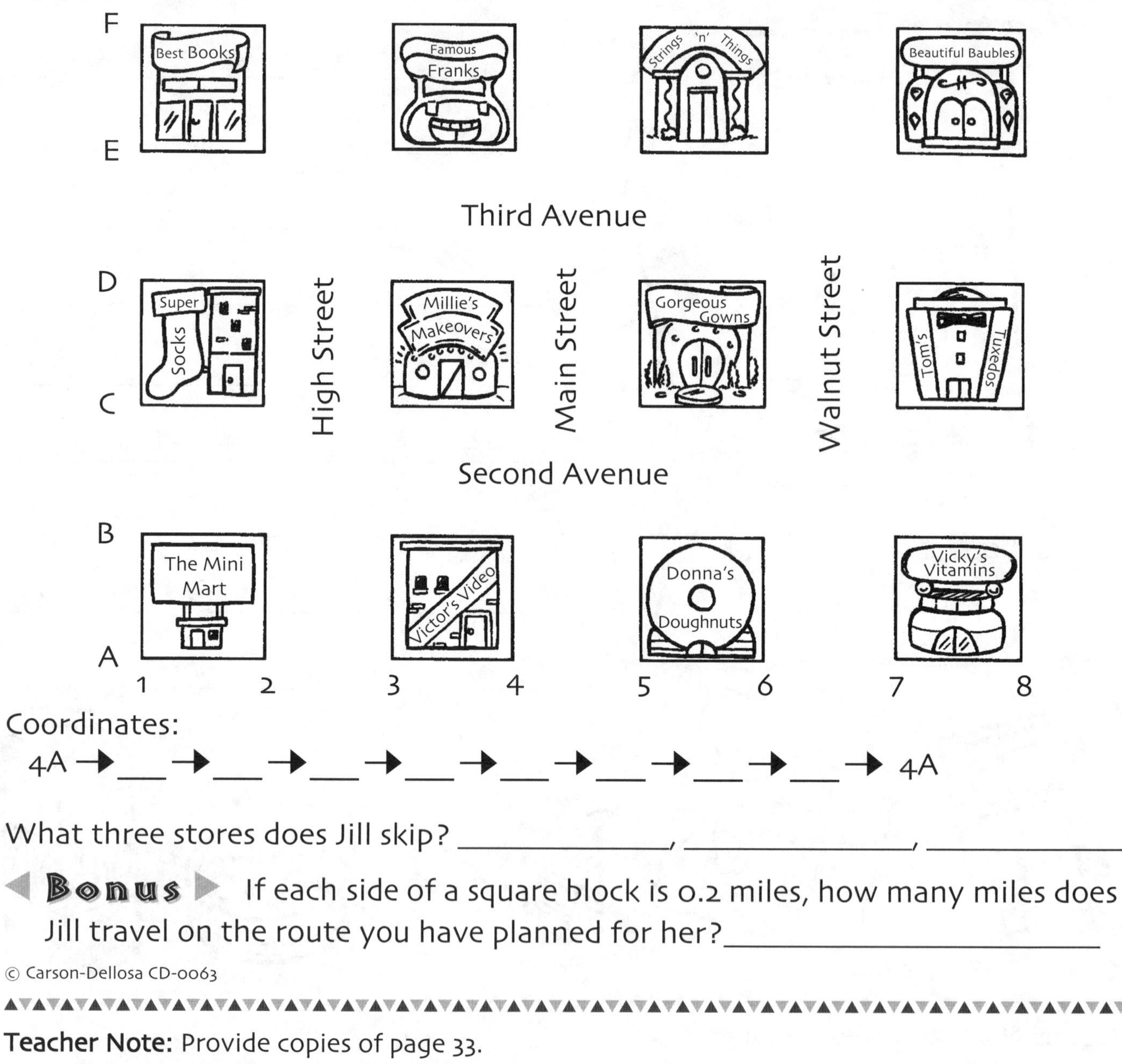

Coordinates:

4A → ___ → ___ → ___ → ___ → ___ → ___ → ___ → ___ → 4A

What three stores does Jill skip? ______________, ______________, ______________

Bonus If each side of a square block is 0.2 miles, how many miles does Jill travel on the route you have planned for her? ____________________

Teacher Note: Provide copies of page 33.

Name ______________________ Date ______________

A Look at the Past

Directions There are many items we use every day that didn't even exist one hundred years ago: computer, cell phone, pager, microwave oven, etc. Make a list below of at least twenty-five things we have today that people didn't have one hundred years ago. Then, write a paragraph on the lines below to tell how these things have made an impact on life today.

1. ______________
2. ______________
3. ______________
4. ______________
5. ______________
6. ______________
7. ______________
8. ______________
9. ______________
10. ______________
11. ______________
12. ______________
13. ______________
14. ______________
15. ______________
16. ______________
17. ______________
18. ______________
19. ______________
20. ______________
21. ______________
22. ______________
23. ______________
24. ______________
25. ______________

Bonus Choose only five things that you would want to have if you had to do without the rest. Tell why you chose each of the five items.

Name ______________________________ Date ____________________

Walk in Another Person's Shoes

Directions Have you ever wondered what it would be like to be someone else for a day? Think of someone you admire or choose from the list below and pretend that you have one day to walk in his or her shoes.

The president of the United States
The queen of England
The principal of your school
The mayor or head of your town/city
A movie star

Who did you choose? ____

What is the first thing you would want to do? ____________________________

____

On the day-planner page below, identify all of the activities in which you think you would be involved as this other person. Start when you wake up in the morning and end when you go to bed at night.

Time	Monday
8:00	
10:00	
1:00	
3:00	
6:00	
8:00	
11:00	

Bonus Describe the most memorable experience you had as this person and give your reasons why.

Name ______________________ Date ______________

Dino Designs

Directions Thousands of years ago, many different kinds of dinosaurs lived on the earth. Some were huge and ferocious, and others were quite small. Some knew how to swim and others flew. Some had a taste for meat, while others only dined on plants.

There's a good chance that all the types of dinosaurs that lived on the earth have yet to be discovered. Only through geological digs have scientists been able to identify the dinosaurs we know about. Imagine you have just discovered the fossils of a new type of dinosaur. Research these three familiar dinosaurs and write some facts about them below. Then, use that information and some creativity to fill in the facts about your own dinosaur discovery.

Tyrannosaurus rex (carnivore)	**Apatosaurus** (herbivore)	**Pteranodon** (flyer)
______________	______________	______________
______________	______________	______________
______________	______________	______________
______________	______________	______________
______________	______________	______________

Your Dinosaur Discovery:

Name your dinosaur ______________________

Physical features (include height, weight, size, color, texture of skin, other)

____

Habitat (land and climate) ______________________

Diet ______________________

Predators ______________________

Prey ______________________

Other interesting facts ______________________

____

Bonus Draw a picture of your dinosaur and tell how it became extinct.

Name ______________________ Date ______________

My Favorite Breed

Directions Describe a cat or a dog. Select a particular breed and use the categories below to help you list the features about this animal.

My animal is a ______________________________.

head	
eyes	
ears	
muzzle	
teeth	
neck	
size/weight	
body	
tail	
legs	
feet	
color	
hair/fur	
other details	

Bonus Draw a picture of your cat or dog on a ~~separate piece of~~ the back of this paper and post it on a bulletin board in the classroom. Leave your description sheet in a basket nearby. See if your classmates can match your picture to the description.

Teacher Note: Provide books about cats and dogs.

Name ______________________________ Date ____________________

Around the World

Directions Solve the riddles below to take a trip around the world. Then, check your answers using an atlas and the latitude and longitude lines. Be sure to name the city (and state, if appropriate) and the country of each destination. Bon voyage!

1. This city and state use the same name. Latitude = 40°N Longitude = 73°W
2. In this city, everybody wants to be a star. Latitude = 34°N Longitude = 118°W
3. On December 7, 1941, the Japanese attacked a harbor in this city. Latitude = 21°N Longitude = 157°W
4. The name of this city rhymes. Latitude = 22°N Longitude = 114°E
5. This city can be either a boy's or girl's name. Latitude = 30°S Longitude = 151°E
6. In this city, you will find a red square. Latitude = 55°N Longitude = 37°E
7. From this city, you can see the pyramids. Latitude = 29°N Longitude = 31°E
8. This city is where the first Olympic games were held. Latitude = 37°N Longitude = 23°E
9. Gladiators once fought in this city. Latitude = 41°N Longitude = 12°E
10. For the 1889 World's Fair, a steel tower was built in this city. Latitude = 40°N Longitude = 2°E
11. This city is spelled the same way as a bean we eat. Latitude = 12°S Longitude = 77°W
12. We're back to the city and state with the same name. Latitude = 40°N Longitude = 73°W

Bonus Name a popular tourist attraction in each city.

Teacher Note: Provide an atlas.

Name ______________________ Date ______________

Scientist Search

Directions Choose two scientists from the list below. Then, research information about their lives and their accomplishments. On a separate sheet of paper, answer the questions below for the two scientists. Then, use the Venn diagram to compare and contrast the two scientists you have chosen.

Albert Einstein	Alexander Graham Bell	André-Marie Ampère
Marie Curie	Anders Celsius	Rudolf Diesel
Thomas Alva Edison	Count Alessandro Volta	Michael Faraday
Aristotle	Antonie van Leeuwenhoek	James Prescott Joule

1. Where and when did this scientist live?
2. What was his/her childhood like?
3. Did this scientist face any personal obstacles in his/her life?
4. What was this scientist famous for?
5. Did his/her discovery change the way people lived?

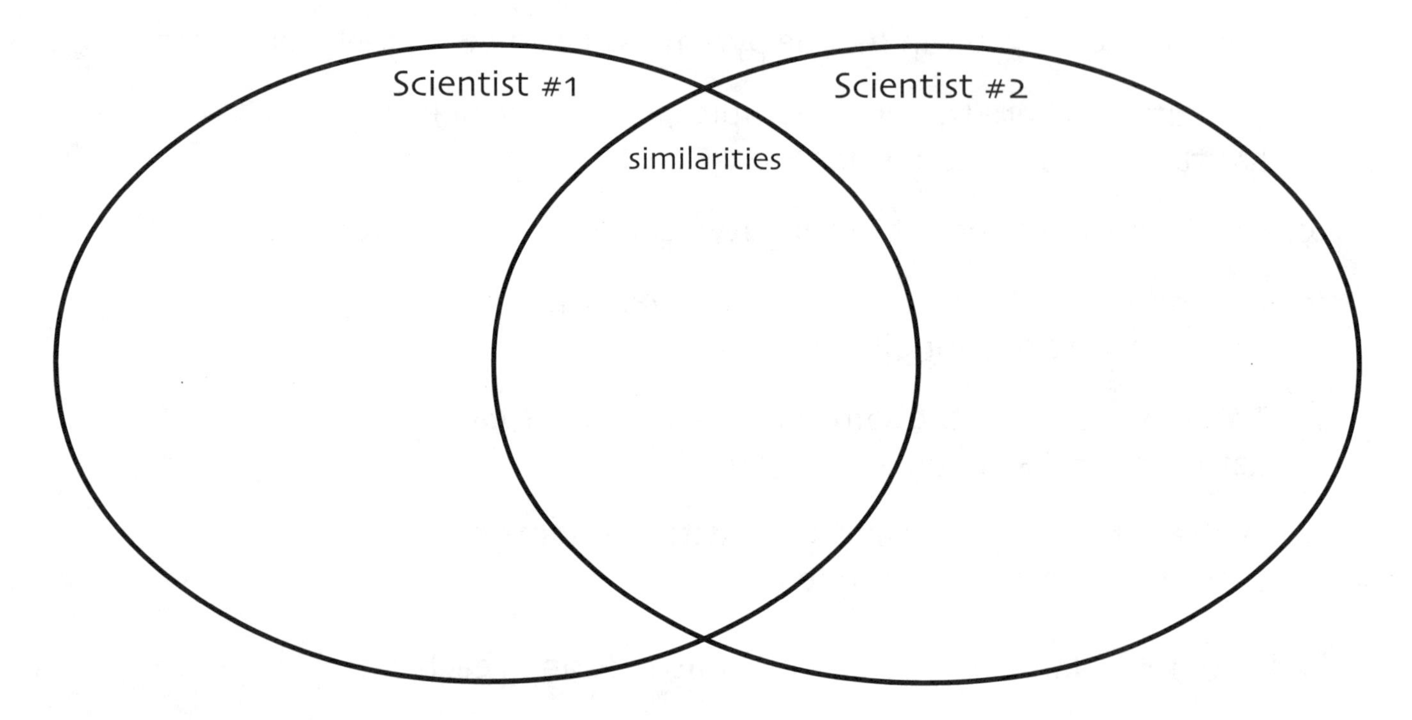

Teacher Note: Provide research materials.

Name ______________________________ Date ____________________

Explorers

Directions Early explorers were very brave. They did not have maps showing them the way like we do now. When they set out to find new lands, it was often a dangerous and frightening adventure.

Below is a list of early explorers. Choose three to research and, on the map below, show which routes each explorer took and how far they were able to travel. Use a different color for each explorer and different types of lines to show if they made more than one voyage. (Ex. ______, _ _ _ _)

Leif Eriksson	Christopher Columbus	Ferdinand Magellan
Juan Ponce de León	Marco Polo	Francisco Pizarro
Hernando Cortés	Bartholomeu Dias	Francisco Coronado
Vasco da Gama	Hernando de Soto	Jacques Cartier
Giovanni Caboto	Amerigo Vespucci	Samuel de Champlain
Vasco Balboa	Jacques Marquette	Prince Henry

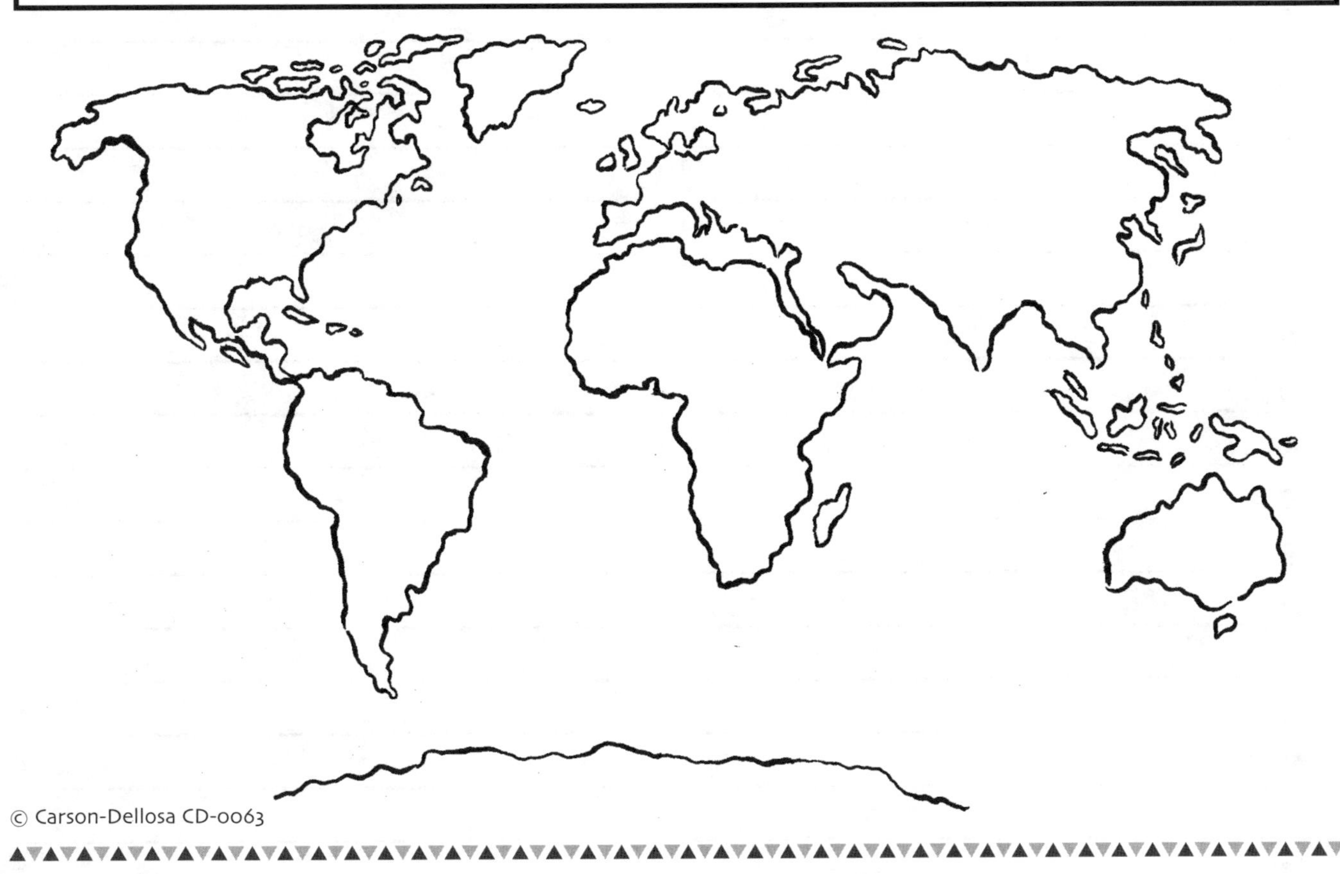

Teacher Note: Provide research materials.

Name ______________________ Date ______________

◀ ABC River Walk ▶

◀ **Directions** ▶ See how many rivers you can name, one for each letter of the alphabet. On the second line after each letter, name the country in which each river is located.

A ______________ ______________
B ______________ ______________
C ______________ ______________
D ______________ ______________
E ______________ ______________
F ______________ ______________
G ______________ ______________
H ______________ ______________
I ______________ ______________
J ______________ ______________
K ______________ ______________
L ______________ ______________
M ______________ ______________
N ______________ ______________
O ______________ ______________
P ______________ ______________
Q ______________ ______________
R ______________ ______________
S ______________ ______________
T ______________ ______________
U ______________ ______________
V ______________ ______________
W ______________ ______________
X ______________ ______________
Y ______________ ______________
Z ______________ ______________

Name ______________________________ Date ____________________

Flower Facts

Directions Complete the flowers below to test your knowledge. The center of each flower has a major topic. List as many facts as you can in the petals of the flower that are related to the topic. The first one is done for you.

Bonus Pick one of the topics and write a paragraph about it, using the facts you wrote on the petals.

Name ______________________________ Date ____________________

Can You Use This?

Directions Recycling used materials is important to the earth and our future. Eventually we could run out of natural resources, such as trees and water. Follow the directions below to help our environment.

- Create a list of things that should be recycled.

1. ____________________ 11. ____________________
2. ____________________ 12. ____________________
3. ____________________ 13. ____________________
4. ____________________ 14. ____________________
5. ____________________ 15. ____________________
6. ____________________ 16. ____________________
7. ____________________ 17. ____________________
8. ____________________ 18. ____________________
9. ____________________ 19. ____________________
10. ____________________ 20. ____________________

- Pick several items and decide how they could be reused.

____
____
____
____
____
____
____
____

- Invent something useful from one or more recycled materials. Create your invention on the back of this paper. (We wouldn't want to waste the back of a perfectly good piece of paper!)

Name ______________________________ Date ____________________

Create a Country

Directions Imagine you have been chosen to be the leader of a new country. You will have many decisions to make as you create your country using your imagination. Use this graphic organizer to help you get started. Use page 46 to complete the assignment.

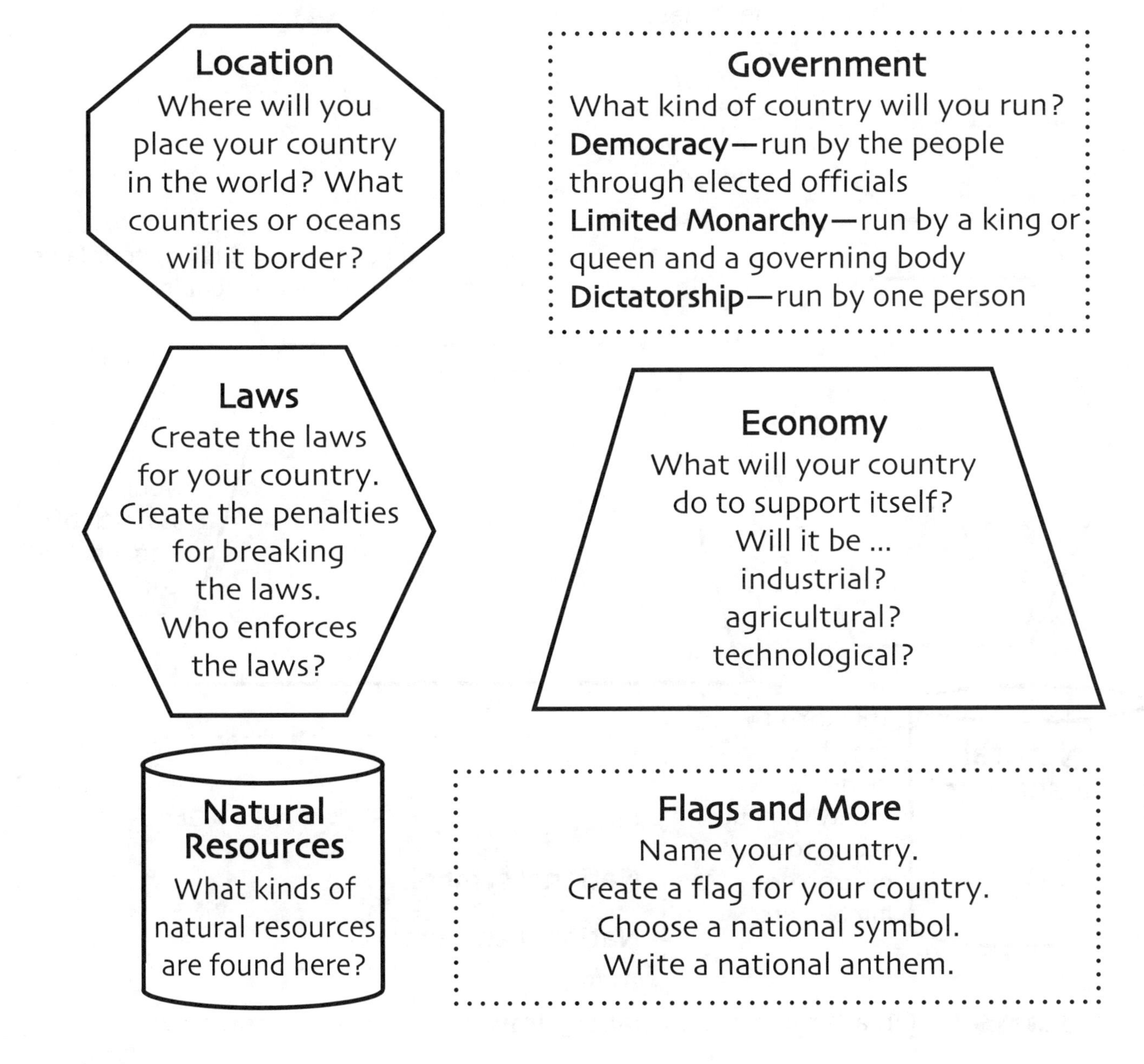

Teacher Note: Provide copies of page 46.

Name ______________________ Date ______________

Create a Country

Directions Use the graphic organizer from page 45 to create your own country. Write your ideas in the boxes below.

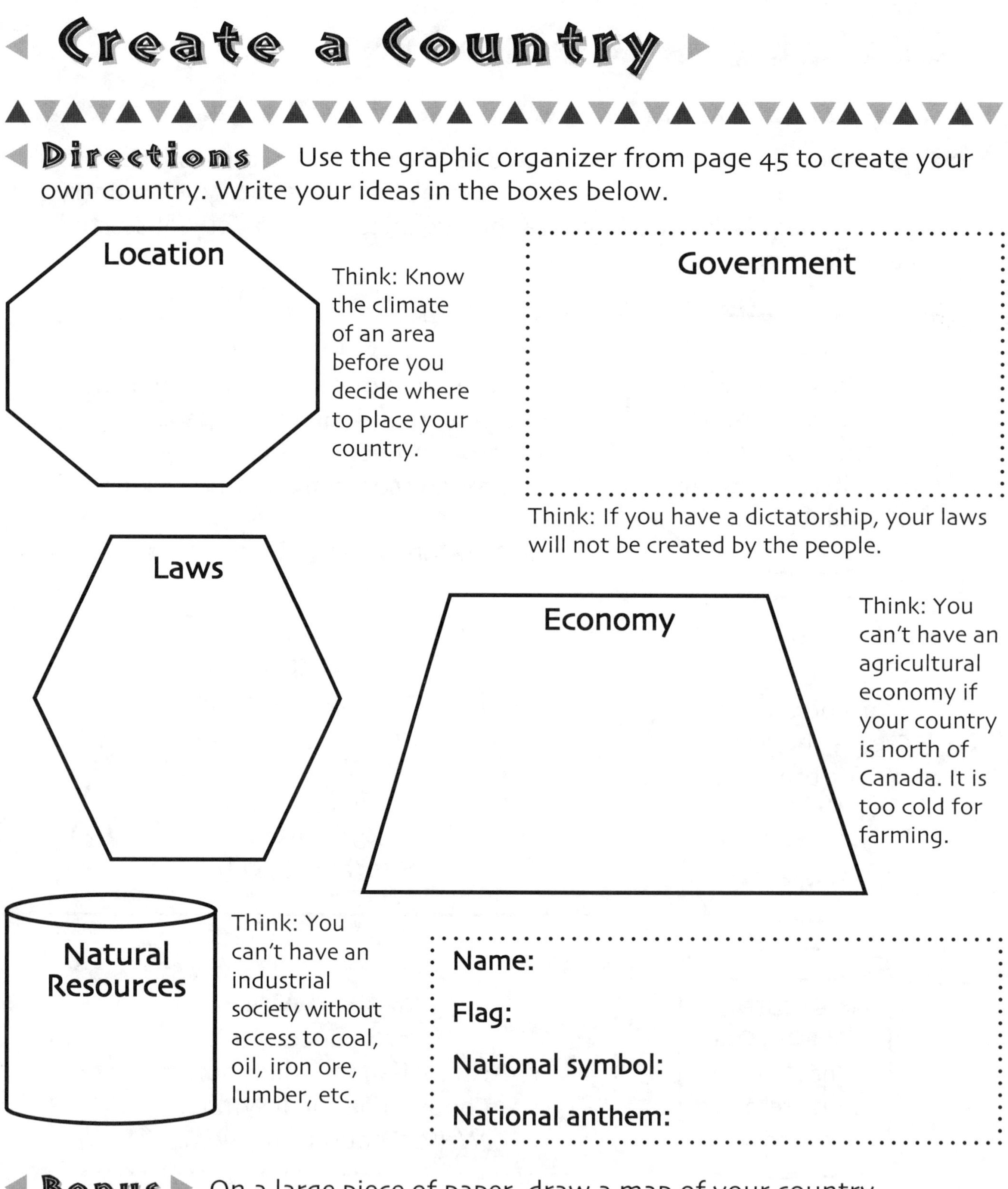

Bonus On a large piece of paper, draw a map of your country.

Teacher Note: Provide copies of page 45.

Name ______________________ Date ______________

Be Brief

Directions Did you ever notice that some things have more than one name? Many things are given an abbreviated name to identify them more quickly in conversation. For example, a refrigerator may be called a fridge.

Fill in the blanks below with the abbreviated version of each word.

frankfurter ______________

mathematics ______________

telephone ______________

airplane ______________

submarine ______________

automobile ______________

examination ______________

tuxedo ______________

jetliner ______________

television ______________

laboratory ______________

bicycle ______________

gymnasium ______________

textbook ______________

Now, try to name the complete word for each of the following shortcuts.

stats ______________

limo ______________

bio ______________

gent ______________

reps ______________

E-mail ______________

pro ______________

legit ______________

ad ______________

zoo ______________

gas ______________

photo ______________

Bonus Make a list of other abbreviated words you can think of.

Name ______________________ Date ______________

Creative Design

Directions Have a little fun. Use your imagination and think outside the box by imagining 10 different uses for each of the following items.

a tissue	a box	a pencil	a rock
______	______	______	______
______	______	______	______
______	______	______	______
______	______	______	______
______	______	______	______
______	______	______	______
______	______	______	______
______	______	______	______
______	______	______	______
______	______	______	______

a spoon	a piece of yarn	a stick	a balloon
______	______	______	______
______	______	______	______
______	______	______	______
______	______	______	______
______	______	______	______
______	______	______	______
______	______	______	______
______	______	______	______
______	______	______	______
______	______	______	______

Name ______________________________ Date ____________________

It's a Match

Directions Some words just seem to go together like peaches and cream. Some more familiar pairs include nuts and bolts and apples and oranges.

See how many other pairs you can identify by filling in the blanks below. Then, put the numbered letters in numerical order to read a special message about the sets of words.

sticks and __ __[14] __ __ __ __

pins and __ __[3] __ __ __ __ __

horse and __ __ __[6] __ __ __ __ __

soap and __ __ __[1] __ __

pots and __[15] __ __ __

macaroni and __[13] __ __ __ __ __

bacon and __[12] __ __ __

lock and __ __ __[4]

peanut butter and __ __ __[7] __ __

bread and __ __ __ __ __ __[10]

salt and __[8] __ __ __ __ __

knife and __[11] __ __ __

hugs and __ __ __ __ __ __[19]

cup and __ __ __ __ __[9] __

table and __ __[2] __ __ __ __

sugar and __ __ __[17] __ __

hammer and __ __[5] __ __

pencil and __ __[16] __ __ __[18]

The message is:

__ __ __ __   __ __ __   __ __ __ __ __ __ __   __ __ __ __ __

1 2 3 4   5 6 7   8 9 10 11 12 13 14   15 16 17 18 19

Bonus Think of other word pairs and create your own puzzle.

Name ______________________________ Date ____________________

Making Comparisons

Directions Writers often use comparisons to give readers a clearer picture of what they mean when describing a character's actions or behavior.

Example: The man was as <u>dirty as a pig</u> and as <u>sly as a fox</u>.

See how many comparisons you recognize by filling in the correct word.

as wise as an _ _ _

as stubborn as a _ _ ☐ _

as slippery as an _ _ _

as busy as a _ _ ☐

as cold as ☐ _ _

as blind as a _ _ _

as quiet as a _ _ _ ☐ _

as slow as ☐ _ _ _ _ _ _ _ _

as flat as a _ _ _ _ _ _ _ _

as neat as a _ ☐ _

Now, unscramble the boxed letters on the lines below to show the name of the literary devise that an author uses when he or she makes a comparison using like or as.

_____ _____ _____ _____ _____ _____

Bonus Can you come up with comparisons of your own? Here's one to get you started: As snug as a bug in a rug.

Name ______________________________ Date ____________________

◀ Create a Game ▶

◀ **Directions** ▶ List as many games as you can on the lines below. You may include outdoor games, indoor games, and board games. Think about how each game is played. You will notice that each game probably has a set of rules.

Create a game of your own. Decide how your game will be played. How will a team or player win your game? Will it be an outdoor game or a board game?

After you make your decisions, come up with a description of your game and a set of rules to follow. If it is a board game, draw the game board on paper. During free time, play the game with your classmates to see if your plan and rules work. Change your plan if you find some problems. Have fun!

List of games:

__________________________ __________________________
__________________________ __________________________
__________________________ __________________________
__________________________ __________________________
__________________________ __________________________
__________________________ __________________________
__________________________ __________________________

Your game: ____

Indoor, board game, outdoor?: ______________________________

Number of players: ______________________________________

Goal/how to win: ____

How to play: ____

____

____

Rules: ____

____

____

Name ______________________ Date ______________

Fun with Word Searches

Directions Make a list of all of your classmates—first names only. Then, write the names on a piece of graph paper, one letter in each square. You can place the names on the graph paper vertically, horizontally, or diagonally. You can also connect the names that have a common letter. Make a second copy as an answer key, and then write other letters to fill up the whole page. Give your word search to a classmate to try.

Classmates' names: ______________ ______________ ______________

	M							
	I							
J	K							
E	E							
F								
F	R	A	N	K				

Bonus Make up other word searches. You can use the names of states, capital cities, countries, animals, or many other word categories.

Teacher Note: Provide graph paper.

Name ______________________ Date ______________

Name That Tune

Directions Certain words seem to be used over and over again by songwriters. Perhaps it's because they concentrate on special themes, such as love, happiness, dreams, etc.

See if you can name five songs in which each of the following words appear:

Baby	Love	Dreams

Bonus Can you think of other words that appear often in songs? Name them and give them to a friend to play Name That Tune.

Name ______________________________ Date ____________________

Puzzle Fun

Directions Study the pictures below and see if you can name each compound word.

Bonus Try to come up with your own compound word pictures.

Name ______________________________ Date ____________________

Can You Find It?

Directions Can you find all of the words from the Word Bank in the puzzle below? When you do, the first few letters left over will reveal a secret message. Starting at the first unused letter, write the letters in order on the lines below until the lines are filled. Good luck!

```
R E I N C R E D I B L E I N T
V O L E N T I O N S W F X E E
E E T I X A F D T S U M L J L
E N Z A B Z E V L H D E L E C
N I M M R O Q V M J V X R C Y
O R E I J E M S A I X B A R C
H A A Y C R G O S H D L W E R
P M R B E R D I T L C F E T O
E B E E G G O Q R U Q E N U T
L U M E B N L W L F A E A P O
E S A P D K I A A T E S L M M
T A C E V R T Z S V J R P O J
J E E R A O L B M S E S R C Y
C B B U R A D M Q J E H I K X
T Y P E W R I T E R R S A M A
```

Word Bank

AIRPLANE	MICROWAVE
AUTOMOBILE	MOTORCYCLE
BEEPER	REFRIGERATOR
CALCULATOR	SUBMARINE
CAMERA	TELEPHONE
COMPUTER	TELEVISION
EYEGLASSES	TYPEWRITER
FAX	

___ ___ ___ ___ ___ ___ ___ ___ ___ ___

___ ___ ___ ___ ___ ___ ___ ___ ___ ___

Name ______________________ Date ______________

Geography Quiz

Directions Using the letters in the word GEOGRAPHY, make a list of geographical terms that are important to know when studying the earth.

Example: G: geomorphology, globe, grid, gulfs

G: ______________________

E: ______________________

O: ______________________

G: ______________________

R: ______________________

A: ______________________

P: ______________________

H: ______________________

Y: ______________________

Bonus Do you know your galactic address? Enter it below.

Street address:

Town, province, or city:

State and/or country:

Continent:

Hemisphere:

Planet:

Name ______________________________ Date ____________________

Acronyms Aplenty

Directions Acronyms are initial letters used to stand for special phrases. You'd be surprised at how many acronyms you can recognize. Do you know what ASAP means? If you guessed "as soon as possible," you are correct. See how many acronyms you can identify below.

USA ______________________	UFO ______________________
NASA ______________________	EPA ______________________
NATO ______________________	FBI ______________________
CIA ______________________	IRS ______________________
ATM ______________________	PIN ______________________
IQ ______________________	TLC ______________________
COD ______________________	MADD™ ______________________
RDA ______________________	AWOL ______________________
WWW ______________________	YMCA® ______________________
PGA™ ______________________	NFL™ ______________________
POW ______________________	MSG ______________________
IOU ______________________	ESP ______________________
ETA ______________________	RIP ______________________

Here's a very special acronym to help you remember the colors in a rainbow. See if you can use it to name the colors.

ROY G BIV

________ ________ ________ ________ ________ ________ ________

Make up an acronym to help you remember something important.

Name ______________________________ Date ____________________

Crack the Code

Directions Use your math reasoning skills to crack the code below. Figure out what numerals are represented by each symbol.

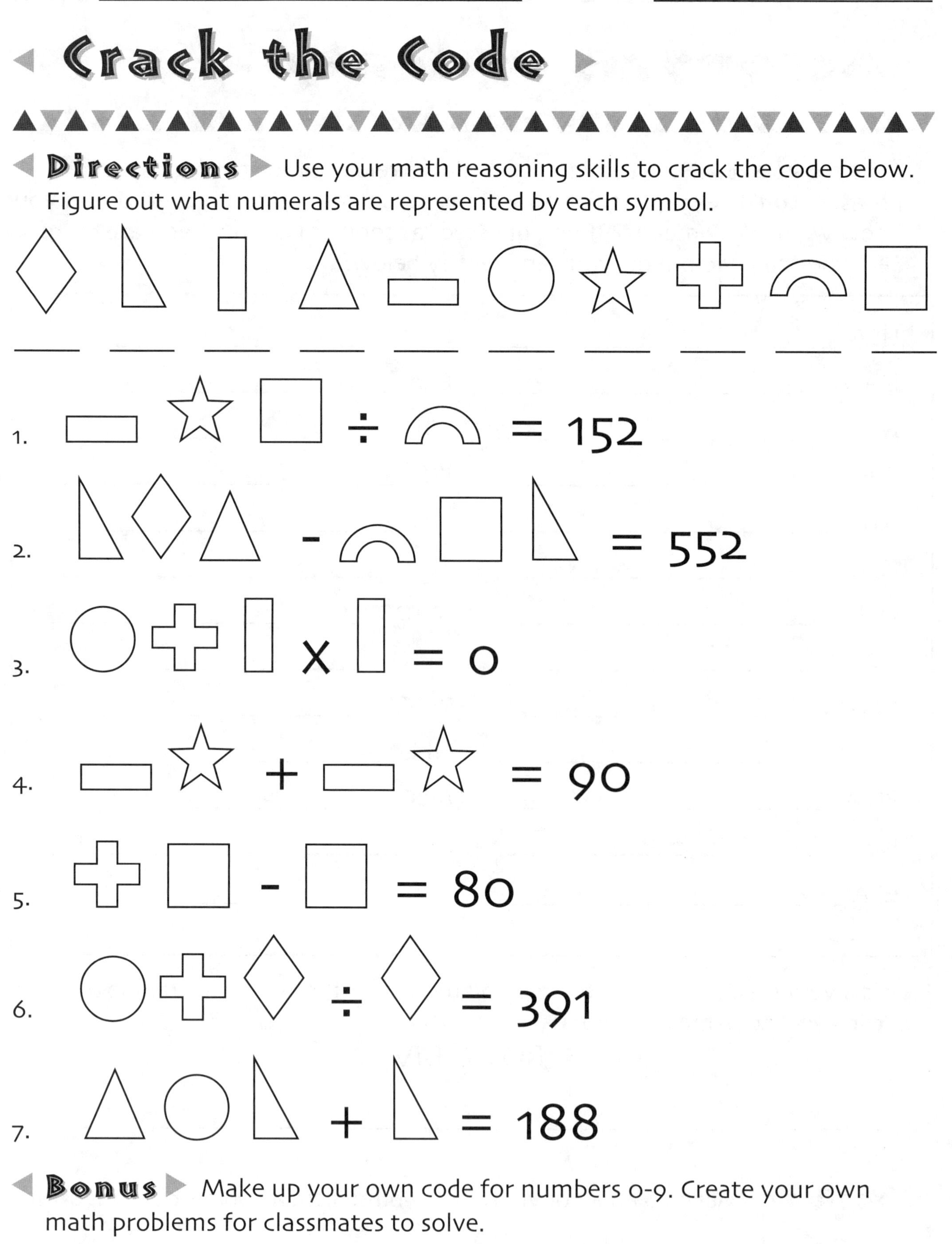

1. ÷ = 152
2. - = 552
3. x = 0
4. + = 90
5. - = 80
6. ÷ = 391
7. + = 188

Bonus Make up your own code for numbers 0-9. Create your own math problems for classmates to solve.

Name ______________________________ Date ____________________

Body Parts

Directions Some things have parts with the same name as parts of the body. For example, you have an eye and there is an eye of a storm.

See how many body part names you can match to parts of the things listed below. You can use the words in the Word Bank more than once.

Word Bank				
eye	ear	hand	leg	arm
teeth	feet	neck	head	face

lettuce ______________________

clock ______________________

table ______________________

chair ______________________

potato ______________________

comb ______________________

corn ______________________

yardstick ______________________

nail ______________________

cube ______________________

bottle ______________________

needle ______________________

Use the space below to draw the items listed above. Draw each object as or with the human body part it has. For example, draw a head of lettuce as a person's head or a comb with human teeth!

Name ______________________________ Date ____________________

Who Said It?

Directions There are hundreds of famous quotes from people all over the world. Below you will find a list of quotes and another list of their authors. Write the number of the quote beside the name of the person who said it. Think about the meaning of the quote before you try to match it, and think about the people who would have reason to write something like that. When you get stuck, use the Internet or an encyclopedia to help you.

1. "A house divided against itself cannot stand."
2. "Ask not what your country can do for you; ask what you can do for your country."
3. "In the middle of difficulty lies opportunity."
4. "If you can DREAM it, you can DO it."
5. "If a man does his best, what else is there?"
6. "The cautious seldom err."
7. "No act of kindness, no matter how small, is ever wasted."
8. "Early to bed and early to rise makes a man healthy, wealthy, and wise."
9. "To be prepared for war is one of the most effectual means of preserving peace."
10. "Give me liberty or give me death!"
11. "You write to me that it's impossible; the word is not French."
12. "I have a dream."

Martin Luther King, Jr.

Benjamin Franklin

Napoleon Bonaparte

George Washington

Patrick Henry

Abraham Lincoln

John F. Kennedy

Aesop

Confucius

Albert Einstein

General George S. Patton

Walt Disney

Bonus Choose three quotes to research where and when they were said.

Name ______________________ Date ______________

Symbol and Frame Game

Directions See how many of the puzzles you can solve by figuring out the meaning of each set of symbols and words.

	read		2B or ~~2B~~	MOON / MIAMI	ccrroossss	Funny Funny Words Words Words Words
Laughing [Crying]	Fork / the $ $ $ $	MIND / MATTER	Close Close Comfort Comfort Comfort Comfort	ꓭ B A A Ↄ C ꓘ K
hahandnd	you J U S T me	school	PAINS	Think [ ]
chair	HOUR	F ꟻ A A C Ↄ E Ǝ	PPRETNYK	skating thin ice

Bonus Try to make up your own word puzzles.

1.				
2.				
3.				
4.				
5.				
6.				
7.				
8.				
9.				
10.				
11.				
12.				
13.				
14.				
15.				
16.				
17.				
18.				
19.				
20.				
21.				
22.				
23.				
24.				
25.				
26.				
27.				

Teacher Note: Use this chart for any activity requiring students to record their responses.

Answer Key

Page 18
car: automobile, buggy
book: tome, volume
birth: beginning, start
trip: journey, expedition
smart: intelligent, sharp
teach: educate, instruct
nice: congenial, pleasant
bad: putrid, decayed
answer: reply, respond
mad: irate, angry
picture: depiction, portrayal

Page 23
S=8, A=6, R=7, U=13, H=20, E=56, K=31, O=4, Y=12, G=33, P=15, T=11, Z=14, I=61, N=10, B=18, D=2, L=9, C=17, M=19
•AN IGLOO •A HOLE

Page 24

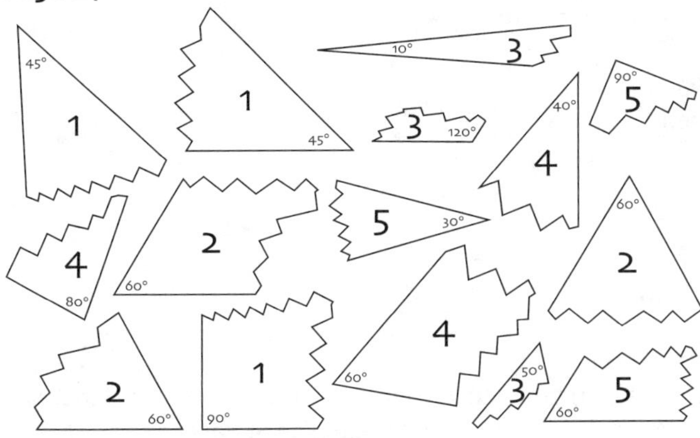

Right, Isosceles, Scalene, Equilateral

Page 25
24; 802; 6,008 = 6,834
21; 108; 4,188; 11,322 = 15,639
36; 124; 1,816 = 1,976
15; 105; 10,485 = 10,605
132; 6,060; 16,002 = 22,194
63; 108; 2,484; 9,000; 18,468 = 30,123
680; 4,430; 10,820 = 15,930
•103,301

Page 26
122 yd.

Page 27
One possible solution: 5 + 50 + 50 ÷ 15 x 11 + 35 – 10 – 2 x 1 = 100

Page 28
triangle, trapezoid, rectangle;
parallelogram, square, rhombus (or parallelogram);
circle, rectangular prism, cylinder, cube;
diamond (or rhombus or parallelogram), octagon, pentagon

Page 29
square: princess poster or frames to left of clock
triangle: princess's hat
product: the answer to problem #2
addend: one of the numbers being added together in problem #1
diameter: 10" line across the circle on the board
rectangle: "stop" poster or chalkboard
median: 83 in grades list
equal sign: "=" in C x D = π
subtrahend: 482 in problem #3
sphere: globe
mean: 81.57 beside grades list
symbol: π
congruent: square posters at top left
octagon: stop sign on the poster
acute angle: hands on the clock
percent: % beside the average grade
parallel: any two vertical or horizontal lines
sum: the answer to problem #1

Page 31
addend, borrow, congruent, data, equation, factor, graph, hexagon, infinity, join, kilogram, length, mean, number, odd, parallel, quotient, radius, solution, tessellation, unit, vertex, weight, x-axis, yard, zero

Page 32
$^1/_2$ of a head of lettuce
1 cup of black olives
$^2/_3$ of an apple
$^4/_7$ of a carrot
$^3/_4$ of a green pepper
1 $^1/_2$ tomatoes
$^1/_2$ of a cup of croutons
$^4/_9$ of a cucumber

Pages 33-34
Victor's Video (4A), Donna's Doughnuts (5A), Gorgeous Gowns (5C), Strings 'n' Things (5E), Beautiful Baubles (7E), Famous Franks (4E), Best Books (2E), Super Socks (2C), The Mini Mart (2A), return to 4A
•Vicky's Vitamins, Tom's Tuxedos, Millie's Makeovers
• 3.6 miles

Answer Key

Page 39

1. New York, New York; USA
2. Hollywood, California; USA
3. Oahu, Hawaii; USA
4. Hong Kong; China
5. Sydney; Australia
6. Moscow; Russia
7. Cairo; Egypt
8. Athens; Greece
9. Rome; Italy
10. Paris; France
11. Lima; Peru
12. New York, New York; USA

Page 47

frank, math, phone, plane, sub, auto, exam, tux, jet, TV, lab, bike, gym, book;
statistics, limousine, biography, gentleman, representatives, electronic-mail, professional, legitimate, advertisement, zoological park, gasoline, photograph

Page 49

stones, needles, carriage, water, pans, cheese, eggs, key, jelly, butter, pepper, fork, kisses, saucer, chairs, spice, nail, paper • they are perfect pairs

Page 50

owl, mule, eel, bee, ice, bat, mouse, molasses, pancake, pin • simile

Page 54

pocketbook, cupcake, cornflower, toenail, popcorn, springboard, hourglass, eyeglasses, rainbow

Page 55

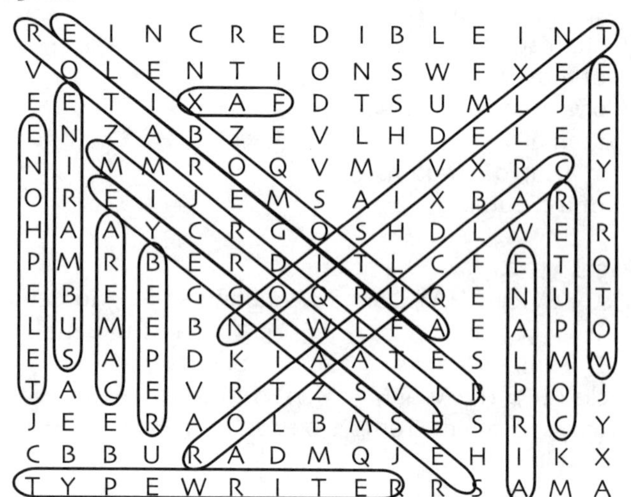

Page 57

United States of America; National Aeronautics and Space Administration; North Atlantic Treaty Organization; Central Intelligence Agency, automated teller machine; intelligence quotient; cash on delivery; recommended daily allowance; World Wide Web, Pro Golf Association™, prisoner of war; I owe you; estimated time of arrival; unidentified flying object; Environmental Protection Agency; Federal Bureau of Investigation; Internal Revenue Service; personal identification number; tender loving care; Mothers Against Drunk Driving™, absent without leave; Young Men's Christian Association®, National Football League™, monosodium glutamate; extrasensory perception; rest in peace
• red, orange, yellow, green, blue, indigo, violet

Page 58

(code from left to right) 2, 9, 0, 1, 4, 7, 5, 8, 3, 6
1. 456 ÷ 3; 2. 921 – 369; 3. 780 x 0; 4. 45 + 45; 5. 86 – 6; 6. 782 ÷ 2; 7. 179 + 9

Page 59

head	ear
hand	feet
leg	head
arm	face
eye	neck
teeth	eye

Page 60

1. Abraham Lincoln; 2. John F. Kennedy; 3. Albert Einstein; 4. Walt Disney; 5. General George S. Patton; 6. Confucius; 7. Aesop; 8. Benjamin Franklin; 9. George Washington; 10. Patrick Henry; 11. Napoleon Bonaparte; 12. Martin Luther King, Jr.

Page 61

(from left to right and top to bottom) read between the lines; "To be or not to be"; Moon over Miami; double cross; too funny for words; laughing on the outside, crying on the inside; Fork over the money; mind over matter; too close for comfort; back to back; hand in hand; just between you and me; high school; growing pains; Think outside the box; high chair; half an hour; face to face; pretty in pink; skating on thin ice